Th

BRILL

I wonder how long
someone can live
without a brain.

How old are you?

BRILL was devised by Ian Rosenbloom and is copyright Yorkshire Television.

**YORKSHIRE
TELEVISION**

Production team:

Paul Walker, Jon Stephens, Yvonne Mellor, Judith Rose, Liz Bowler, Camilla Wheeler

Executive Producer:

Ian Rosenbloom

*Hodder
Children's
Books*

Published by Hodder Children's Books 1995

Written by Vic Parker

Inside artwork by Alan Rowe

ISBN 0 340 646519

Printed by Cox and Wyman

Hodder Children's Books is a division of Hodder Headline plc, 338 Euston Road London NW1 3BH

Foreword

When my agent called to tell me that I'd got the job, I knew it was too good to be true.

'Trying out loads of BRILL things and getting paid for it?!' I squealed in excitement. 'This'll show my careers teacher! She once told me that I was such a couch potato that the only job I was fit for was testing sofas...'

'Actually, John,' I heard my embarrassed agent reply. 'They were looking for a couch potato. And there's one little snag. Your co-presenter is a flatfish.'

Well as if that wasn't bad enough, I now find myself sharing a book with it.

Anyway, learning how to be BRILL at everything from making pizza to karting has been well worth all the trouble with marine wildlife. And now it's your turn.

John Eccleston

PS
I know that 'BRILL' is a snappier name than 'John Eccleston', but I must say that I object to the fish getting star billing...

Be **BRILL** at keeping exotic pets

There are loads of absolutely BRILL exotic animals you can keep at home as pets. But the main thing to remember is that all pets - exotic or not - need a great deal of looking after, and this will be up to YOU! So if you're as bad as I am at everyday jobs like making your bed and brushing your teeth, maybe it's not a good idea to get a pet - which will need regular care too.

Here are some things to think about when you're choosing an exotic pet:

How much money do you want to spend on your pet and its upkeep?

It's best to start off with a pet that's fairly cheap, and which doesn't need alot of expensive equipment or food. If you get dead BRILL at keeping exotic pets, you can always save up for something more expensive, like a Mexican Red Kneed spider at around £70. On the other hand, if you're as rich as Michael Jackson, there are loads of REALLY expensive exotic pets - like a £70,000 carp!

How big will your pet grow?

Don't forget that cute little baby exotic pets grow into whopping great adult exotic pets! If you just can't resist that soppy-eyed iguana with the waggly tail,  remember that in a couple of years' time you might find yourself spending all your pocket money on food for your very hungry, 2 metre-long pet. And don't blame me if your mum says that she was quite fond of your corn snake when it was a baby, but now that it's four feet long it's going to have to go!

What does your pet live on?

Most exotic pets live on other animals, like worms, crickets and mice. You can buy them from pet shops - but you should ask yourself honestly whether you'll mind hand-feeding live animals to your exotic pet. You can get around this by buying them frozen, but you'll still have to warm them up to body temperature and wiggle them around in front of your pet. It might also be an idea to ask your mum if she minds you keeping your dead mice in her freezer, as she may not be that keen ...

How difficult is your pet going to be to keep?
And is it dangerous?

If you don't keep your pet at the right temperature, in the right kind of housing, with the right kind of food - it won't last very long! This will be very sad for both you and your pet, so make sure you have enough space, money and time to be able to keep your pet happy. You also need to find out whether or not your pet is dangerous, and if so, what precautions you need to take.

Why not join a group of exotic animal enthusiasts? If there isn't one near where you live, start one yourself!

How to get dead BRILL at ice skating

Take it from me, the hardest thing about learning to skate is the ice. Unfortunately, I learned this through painful experience. But if you can get over this, you're half-way there.

How to start

The best way to start is to take a class. This way, you won't pick up bad habits, so you'll get BRILL at ice skating faster. Check your local phone book to find out which is your nearest rink, or you could try your local sports centre for details.

What you WON'T need

1 One of those skin-tight suits with flarey trousers or a leotard with an itsy-bitsy-teeny-weeny skirt
It's not very pleasant to keep sitting down with only the thinnest layer of lycra between you and the very cold ice rink, so it's best to wear layers of loose, comfortable clothes which will keep you warm and also allow you to move easily. You

should also wear gloves. These aren't just to keep your hands warm, they're also to protect you when you fall over (and even experts do this sometimes).

2 Your own ice skates

Most people hire ice skates from the ice rink. Don't be afraid to try different sizes of skates if the ones you're given don't feel comfortable at first - learning in uncomfortable skates can be a real pain.

TIPS FOR BEING BRILL

1 Make sure you remove the plastic guards from the blades of your skates (if they have any). I didn't, and I didn't get very far.

2 Try to hold the barrier at arm's length. If you can stop yourself from clinging on for dear life with both hands, you'll build up confidence quicker.

3 Don't be embarrassed about falling over. Remember that everyone has to start somewhere! Even Torvill and Dean must have fallen over a good few times before managing their first lap.

4 Remember that once you get going, you'll have to have some idea of how you're going to

S....t...o...P!

Amaze your friends with a piece of paper!

Here's an amazing trick that is simple to make, but looks totally baffling. All you need is a sheet of paper that's the same colour and texture on both sides and which doesn't have holes punched along one edge, and a pair of scissors.

1 Make a tiny crease half-way along the long edge of your paper.

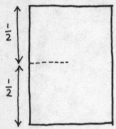

2 Make two tiny creases along the opposite long edge, one-quarter and three-quarters along it.

3 Cut along the half-way mark and the two quarter marks on the opposite edges of the paper. Make sure that you cut to the mid-point of the paper.

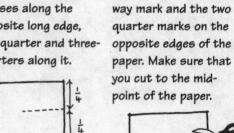

4 Twist the top of the sheet of the paper around by one half turn.

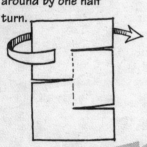

AN EASY WAY TO ANNOY SOMEONE IS TO SHOW THEM YOUR ILLUSION AND CHALLENGE THEM TO MAKE IT THEMSELVES!

A rectangle, which looks as though it's grown from nothing, should now stand out of the flat sheet of paper.

Did you know?

Did you know that the Denby Dale Pie holds the record for the largest ever meat pie? It was baked in September 1988 and weighed an incredible 19,908 lb. The people of Denby Dale in Yorkshire first baked a huge pie over 200 years ago, to celebrate King George III's recovery from madness. If you ask me, they were more mad than he was!

Be a dead BRILL practical joker

The main ingredient for successful practical joking is SURPRISE. Most people aren't as completely stupid as my Auntie Mavis and soon catch on if you start using up all of your BRILL practical jokes on them. If you set out to annoy your family and friends while they're waiting for you to try something, all that will happen is that YOU'LL get annoyed instead.

This is unbelievably frustrating, as it often takes time and effort to set up the best tricks.

The other important thing is to make sure that your practical jokes don't backfire. If your victim doesn't have a sense of humour they won't appreciate how BRILL your practical joke was. This is their problem, not yours, but it might get you into trouble all the same. On the other hand, if your practical joke doesn't work, you might end up in a highly unpleasant situation which is entirely of your own making! (And I should know, it was my fault that I had to spend a whole week on holiday in sunny Bognor Regis with good old Auntie Mavis).

Make sure you don't end up with egg on your face!

There are some good joke shops around which stock all kinds of instant practical joke. Why not offer hungry guests rubber sausages, bananas or toast, strategically place a plastic spider in someone's bath or bed, or turn your victim's face black with trick soap or binoculars?

But there are loads of DIY practical jokes you can try without forking out for any special equipment. Over the page, you'll find some of my favourites.

The sugar and salt swap swizz

This one never fails. Empty the sugar bowl and fill it with salt instead, putting the sugar into the empty salt cellar. Then wait until someone reaches for the sugar or salt, sit back and watch their face. (Make sure you remember what you've done, though. This isn't as silly as it sounds ...)

BRILL TIP: YOU CAN ALSO DO THIS WITH CURRY POWDER INSTEAD OF PEPPER, AND A GENEROUS HELPING OF MUSTARD INSTEAD OF CUSTARD. MMMM! YUMMY!

The old soak

Fill an empty plastic bottle with tap water and screw the top on tightly. With a pin, make some tiny holes around the bottle, near the bottom. (As long as you screwed the top on tightly, the water won't come out.) Ask a friend if they'd like a drink, and give them the bottle without opening it. When your friend unscrews the top to take a drink, the water will spurt out through the holes at the bottom and soak them!

A great shake

If you know you're going to have to shake hands with someone, or suspect that some relative you hardly know is going to try to hold your hand, why not make sure that you've got a few mushy grapes or a big dollop of gunk in your palm? (That'll soon stop Aunty Mavis from planting a big kiss on your mooey and commenting on how you've grown.)

Bottoms up!

You'll need to be extra-specially cunning to pull this one off, but it's completely **BRILL** if you manage it. Creep up behind someone, without them seeing you. (This is the hard part - you might need a partner in crime to hold your victim's attention somehow.)

Gently clip a long piece of loo roll onto their skirt or trousers with a clothes peg, then time how long it takes for someone to pluck up enough courage to tell your victim the embarrassing truth!

A gotcha for the greedy

All you need is a fairly long stick, some thread, a five pound note, and someone who can never resist an easy way to get some money. Attach the fiver to the stick by means of a long piece of the thread, then retreat to a safe hiding place. Dangle the fiver in the open, and wait for a gullible sucker to try to pick it up ... then quickly whip it a little further away from them. They're bound to walk over to it and try to pick it up again ... I'm sure you've cottoned on. (Geddit?)

Conned by computer

If you've got access to a computer, it won't take long to produce an official-looking letter announcing that your victim has won an amazing prize in a competition. (Watch out what the prize is with this one, though. This is how I ended up having to go on holiday with the dreaded Aunty Mavis ...)

Put on a **BRILL** show

Have you ever had the urge to put on your own show ? Well, why don't you? You don't need a theatre, you can perform just about anywhere - your garage, a community centre, your school hall. Anywhere it's possible to get an audience in!

> Luvvie, what's 25 ft long, ugly and sings 'Scotland the Brave'?
> The Loch Ness Songster!

Don't forget that you won't just need performers, you'll also need clothes for dressing up in, bits of make-up, props and maybe even some scenery too. So everyone can play a part, even if they don't want to perform. Car boot sales and charity shops are good places to look for costumes and props. Beg, borrow, but don't steal!

Make-up is easy to get hold of. Someone in your family is bound to have some - but make sure you ask first. I know it's tempting just to go ahead and take your older sister's new and amazingly expensive Christian Dior lipstick - or use her clothes for a Dame Edna Everage costume, for that matter - but you won't be very popular for quite a while if you do. So don't say you haven't been warned!

It doesn't matter if you're putting on a show in your living room or in a 500 seat theatre, the golden rules are still the same:

You need to be very clear and precise, so your audience can hear what you're saying and see what you're doing.

Project your personality, so you catch the attention of your audience and make them want to continue watching you.

Don't try and do too much! It's better to have a quick, utterly BRILL show, than a long, extremely boring show.

If you feel that your main talent is treading the boards, why not join a drama club or youth theatre? Don't forget that youth theatres always need help with costumes and make-up, scenery and props, and sound and lighting too, besides which, there also has to be someone to direct the whole thing.

— STARFISH —

One of William Shakespeare's most infamous plays is about the Scottish king Macbeth. But did you know that superstitious actors think it's unlucky to say 'Macbeth' in a theatre? To avoid using the name, they refer to it as 'the Scottish play'.

DID YOU ALSO KNOW THAT WHEN FROGS GO TO THE THEATRE, THEY LEAVE THEIR COATS AND HATS IN THE CROAKROOM?

Variety shows as we know them today developed in the 1800s from the Edwardian music halls. These were originally for amateurs to show off their talents (a bit like karaoke!). Americans called this kind of show 'vaudeville', from the French 'voix de ville', which means 'voice of the city'. Acts included singers, comics, high wire acts and golfing demonstrations!

MUSIC HALL MUSSELS

Karting is dead **BRILL**

It doesn't matter how old you are, you don't need a driving licence, and you don't need any previous driving experience - absolutely anyone can be dead **BRILL** at karting ... providing you can reach the pedals, that is. You don't need any special equipment. All you have to do is get along to an indoor karting circuit, and have a go!

(There are also outdoor karting circuits, but to drive on one of these you must be at least 8 years old and hold a Competition Licence with Medical Certificate.)

Karting is a much cheaper alternative to motor racing - and just as exciting! You sit just half an inch from the ground, and can reach speeds ranging from 60 to 160 miles per hour on an outdoor track. The utterly **BRILL** Formula One racing car drivers Alain Prost and Nigel Mansell started their careers in kart racing.

INFO

The first ever kart was built in the mid-1940s by an American called Art Engles, using a lawn mower engine! He had only one pedal - the accelerator (I wonder how he managed to stop?) and tested the kart in car parks. The Go Kart Club of America was formed as interest in karting grew, and the very first organised kart race took place in December 1957 at the Eastland Shopping Centre in Covina, USA.

Sergeant Micky Flynn, a US airman stationed in the north west of England, introduced karts into this country in 1958, and after a demonstration of karts at Silverstone, the first official kart race in England took place in Lakenheath in November 1959.

What swims through the water at 100 miles an hour?

A go-carp

What kind of fish is most useful on an ice rink?
A Skate. Sorry, Brill!

Did you know?

Dame Nellie Melba was a world-famous Australian opera star, with a large voice, and an even larger appetite! Melba Toast was named after her, as was Peach Melba - which is ice-cream with peaches and raspberry sauce.

YUM!

Make a **BRILL** pizza

To make an absolutely BRILL pizza, you'll need:

* half a pint of hand-hot water
* 2 teaspoons of dried yeast
* 1 teaspoon of salt
* 1 lb of plain white flour
* 2 dessertspoonfuls of olive oil
* 2 dessertspoonfuls of tomato purée
* ingredients for toppings

(FUNNILY ENOUGH, HAND-HOT WATER IS WATER THAT'S NOT TOO HOT FOR YOU TO PUT YOUR HAND IN IT! WATCH THAT YOU DON'T BURN YOURSELF TRYING, THOUGH...)

1 Put on some Italian music so you can sing along and get in the right frame of mind. I always find that an opera produces the best results, but see what works for you.

2 Mix the flour, salt and yeast together in a bowl. Add the water and olive oil, and mix everything together to form a soft, but not sticky, dough.

3 Either knead the dough on a lightly floured board, or shove everything into a food processor and mix it up for one minute.

4 Brush the inside of a polythene bag with some olive oil (you'll need a little pastry brush to do this - I tried using an old paint brush that was lying around but it just didn't have the same effect). Put your lump of dough inside the bag and leave it in a warm place to rise for about 20 minutes.

5 While you're waiting for your dough to miraculously grow, preheat the oven to gas mark 6/400°F/200°C and prepare your toppings!

6 You can have as many toppings as you want. If you're as greedy as me, the more the better! Cheese is always a good one to start with. You could also try tomatoes, ham, pineapple, mushrooms, peppers, salami, anchovies, tuna, onions, sweetcorn - whatever you like! Just grate the cheese and chop everything else up into chunks.

7 Check that your dough has risen, then roll it out to a flattish, round shape.

8 Spread the tomato purée around on it, then arrange your toppings over that. Put the whole lot on an oiled baking sheet and put it on the top shelf of the oven for about 12-15 minutes.

BRAIN brainpower!

And here's your starter for 10 points... what's the most powerful computer in the world? The human brain, of course! We still know very little about the brain, and experts claim that we'd be able to amazing things if we only knew how to make the most of our minds. Well, you can start boosting your brainpower by improving your memory.

Remembering names and faces

If you're anything like me, the minute you're told someone's name, you instantly forget it! In fact, the trick is quite simple. Our memories work best with pictures and images rather than words, so focus on a couple of the most obvious characteristics of that person, and turn them into pictures.

For example, if the person's name is Frank, picture them wearing boxing shorts and gloves, like Frank Bruno! Or if you meet someone called Lynne, imagine them shaking hands with Linford Christie. Don't worry about how mad your images are. The more weird you make them, the longer they'll stay in your head.

The same thing works with surnames. You could picture someone with the surname 'Babbit' as having long rabbit's ears and a fluffy tail, to remind you of what their surname sounds like ... You'll soon get the hang of it!

Remembering the sequence of the colours of the rainbow

RED,
ORANGE,
YELLOW,
GREEN,
BLUE,
INDIGO,
VIOLET!

It's easy to remember this when you know how! Just learn the sentence, 'Richard Of York Gave Battle In Vain'. Simple!

Remember the order of the planets away from the Sun

Mercury is
nearest to
the Sun, then
Venus,
Earth,
Mars,
Jupiter,
Saturn,
Uranus,
Neptune,
Pluto.

You can remember this useful gem of information by making up a sentence similar to the one for the colours of the rainbow. This more wacky your sentence is, the more likely you are to remember it. Brill uses a fishy sentence: My Very Elderly Mum Jumped Sideways Under Naughty Plankton!

Pass your history exams the easy way!

Remembering dates involves a bit of work - but it'll be really worth it in the end! You have to remember that 0 stands for the letter O, 1 for A, 2 for B, 3 for C, 4 for D, 5 for E, 6 for F, 7 for G, 8 for H and 9 for I. Then you can turn the numbers in a date into pairs of letters. For example, Anne Boleyn's wedding date, 1533, splits up into 15 - or AE, and 33 - or CC. Then

think of famous people with those initials - Albert Einstein and Charlie Chaplin, say. So we can remember the date 1533 by imagining that Albert Einstein and Charlie Chaplin are having tea with Anne Boleyn, who's wearing her wedding dress!

In France, April Fool's day is known as 'Poisson d'Avril', which means 'April Fish'! The start of the year was April the first until 1564, when the French decided to move it to January the first. After this change, people began to send joke cards and presents on the old date, and it's believed that that's how April Fool's day came about.

In Scotland, April the first is known as April Noddy Day and Gowkie Hunting Day.

But wherever you are on April 1st, don't get caught out! You have to play your April Fool's tricks before midday, or else the joke's on you ...

A 'gowkie' is a cuckoo, by the way.

BRILL blood and gore

Film and TV people have a special name for all their gory effects. They call it 'splatter'! Well, although they have lots of money to splash out on their splatter, you can make your own gruesome creations (that are just as BRILL) with very little dosh.

Fake Blood

Did you know that the most fake blood ever used in a movie was on the horror film 'Brain Dead'? They used a gushing 39,000 litres!

All good joke shops sell fake blood, but you can get larger quantities for less wad if you make it yourself at home. Contrary to popular opinion, ketchup doesn't actually make good squirting blood - although it is good for making wounds, as it's thick but washes off quite well. If you want a good spray of blood, it's best to use water with red food colouring in. (You can always thicken this up a bit by adding a touch of flour.) A word of warning though - this dastardly concoction does stain rather well, so don't get it anywhere near anything you don't want to look permanently splattered!

The vilest vomit

The secret of successful huey is having a good base. Thick, creamy porridge is good - not just because it looks right, but also because it doesn't taste too bad! Add a little bit of yellowy food colouring if you like, to make it look even more disgusting. For that really authentic look, add a handful of peas and also some diced tomatoes and carrots. Even if you hate carrots and haven't eaten them for the last six years or so, there's always bits of diced carrot when you vom.

Throw a **BRILL** fake punch

The trick to throwing an utterly convincing fake punch is to place your subject somewhere so that your audience can't see that you're actually missing their face (hopefully). If you hit your chest at the same time as you swing your punch past your victim, you also get exactly the right sound.

To create a realistic cracked teeth effect, crunch up some mints in your mouth during the lead up to the fight, and then spit them out at a suitable moment. You can also get some blood capsules from your local joke shop, hide them in your mouth, and bite into them when you want to add a bit of blood-laced spit to the proceedings.

Flesh it out!

Soak up some toilet paper with water, red food colouring and a little strawberry ice cream syrup. An unlikely combination, you may think! But if you mash this all up into a ball you'll find you have instant flesh ... dead BRILL for making them gasp in horror at severed limbs or buckets of brains, and perfect for splattering liberally over walls!

30

INFO

Some people just aren't satisified with playing practical jokes once a year, on April the first. Horace de Vere Coe, also known as the King of Hoaxers, was born in 1881. For one of his most famous tricks, he posed as a workman and dug a huge hole right in the middle of Piccadilly Circus. The police helpfully diverted all the traffic around the site!

Canoeing is dead BRIL

S ea kayaking is one of the world's earliest forms of water transport, dating as far back as 5000 BC. Today, there are hundreds of canoe clubs all over Britain, and absolutely anyone can have a go. The only slight hitch you might come across is that it's a good idea to learn how to swim first!

What most people think of as canoeing is in fact kayaking, as kayaks have closed tops whereas canoes are open topped. It was the Eskimos who thought of closing the tops of their canoes - they used to sew themselves into their kayaks! This brilliant idea not only stopped water leaking into the boat, it also trapped air inside, making the boat practically unsinkable. However, it also threw up a teeny problem - you couldn't get out of your kayak! Not to be put off, those clever Eskimos invented a way of rolling their kayaks the right way up when they capsized, which surprisingly enough became known as the 'Eskimo roll'!

LEARNING AN ESKIMO ROLL TAKES QUITE A BIT OF PRACTICE!

There are many types of canoe and kayak and lots of different paddling environments. Swimming pools, seas, rivers and lakes all have their own particular hazards and demand their own special paddling skills. Indoor canoe polo is a rapidly growing sport, where two teams of five-a-side try to score by shooting a ball at a goal hung 2 metres above the water. If you're even more adventurous, you could also try canoe surfing, or even white water kayaking! (I'm quite content with just paddling around a swimming pool, myself...)

INFO

Britain's most BRILL ice skaters have been John Curry, Robin Cousins and the partners Jayne Torvill and Christopher Dean. Torvill and Dean won the Olympic Ice Dance Gold Medal in 1984 with the utterly BRILL score of nine 6.0s.

Get skating ... it could be you next!

Did you know?

Did you know that the largest fish in the world is the whale shark? It can grow up to 15 metres **long**!

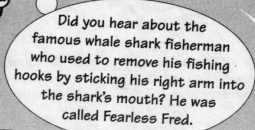

Did you hear about the famous whale shark fisherman who used to remove his fishing hooks by sticking his right arm into the shark's mouth? He was called Fearless Fred.

Was? What's he called now?

Lefty!

An apple pie bed is BRILL

An apple pie bed is a completely **BRILL** way to annoy anyone who has a bed. It doesn't matter whether the victim has sheets and blankets or a duvet. Here's what to do.

1 Take off the duvet or top blankets, so you're left with the undersheet.

2 Take another sheet, just the same, and spread it out over the bed without tucking it in.

3 Pick up the bottom edge of the top sheet and fold it back until it hangs over the top of the bed.

4 Now put the blankets or duvet back on the bed, then fold the overhanging part of the sheet back over them, and tuck it in. Then put the pillow back, so it all looks just like an ordinary bed.

When your tired victim tries to get into their nice, cosy bed, they'll only be able to stretch out their legs half-way down! They'll have to make the whole thing again properly before they can go to sleep.

HERE'S AN UTTERLY BRILL TIP:

IF YOU WANT TO BE ESPECIALLY DASTARDLY, WHY NOT PUT A HAIRBRUSH OR A COLD WATER BOTTLE IN THE BED TOO! IT'S AS EASY AS APPLE PIE...

INFO

In Great Britain, 22 million newspapers are made every single day, and 700 million pounds worth of toilet and tissue paper is bought every year. And that's a lot of people..erm...blowing their noses.

About a third of all waste in your household dustbin is paper, as the average family in Great Britain throws away over 4 kg per week. In many cases, whole forests are cleared to make wood pulp. Look for products that use recycled paper, and try to use every little bit of it.

Did you know?

Did you know that the Aborigines of Australia eat bugs and lizards? And that tarantulas are a delicacy in South East Asia? But the chances are that you've eaten bugs too, as the red food colouring cochineal is made from beetles' wings ...

I love insects!

Yaaargh!

BRILL alternatives to exotic pets

There are loads of bizarre potential pets on your very own doorstep ... well, in your very own garden, anyway. Creepy-crawlies don't cost anything, and you don't have to feed them with disgusting stuff.

> The best way to avoid infection from biting insects is not to bite any!

Just put a jam jar in a hole in the ground, with three stones on top of it, and then a big stone on top of that, to keep the rain out. Leave it all overnight and then go back the next morning to see what you've caught. Use a creepy-crawlies guidebook and a notebook to keep records of what you've found - but don't forget to let your bugs go after you've identified them.

So they think I'm stupid, huh?

Goldfish may not sound very exotic, but in fact they're just as difficult to keep as most exotic pets.

Did you know that goldfish actually have teeth - but at the back of their throats, instead of the front of their mouths. I wonder how long their toothbrushes are . . .?

When you buy a goldfish, you should never put it straight into a tank of water that's just come out of the tap. Always let the water stand for 48 hours first, to get rid of all the chemicals. Then put the goldfish gently into the tank without taking it out of its bag, so that the water inside the bag becomes the same temperature as the water in the tank, and doesn't stress the goldfish. Keep the bag open, to let some air in. After about 2 hours, you can then let the goldfish swim out of its bag and into its new home. Whenever the water begins to get murky, take out about a third of it, and fill up the tank with tap water that has been left to stand for a while.

Goldfish are very particular creatures: they don't like having all their water changed at once, they much prefer square tanks to round ones, and they hate living on their own.

Have you given them some fresh water?

They haven't drunk what I gave them yesterday yet...

Did you know?

In 1865, Scotsman John MacGregor built his own canoe and called it the Rob Roy. He based his design on the kind of canoes used by Native Americans and Eskimos, but with one big difference - he put sails on his, so his arms wouldn't get tired from too much paddling! Talk about being lazy! These days, he'd probably have used an engine...

Blow a **BRILL** raspberry!

All you need to make a really rather BRILL rude noise (some of you will already be able to do this unaided) is a sheet of paper, some sticky tape and a pencil.

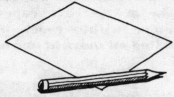

1 Take a sheet of paper and place a pencil on one corner.

2 Roll the paper around the pencil, then hold it in place with a piece of sticky tape. Then tip out the pencil, leaving yourself with an empty paper tube.

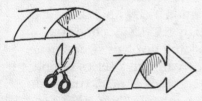

3 Cut one end so that it looks like an arrow head. Make sure that the bottom of the triangle is no longer than 3 or 4 mms, or else you will find yourself making a silent raspberry!

4 Now fold the arrow shape down to cover the end of the tube.

5 Place the other end of the tube in your mouth and suck!

You won't see this on Blue Peter!

43

Skiing is BRILL!

Skiing is dead BRILL - and you don't have to go abroad to try it! There are around 180 artificial ski slopes in the country - most are open all year round, and some are floodlit at night. Look out for special all-day offers, as these are much cheaper than the usual rates. If you're within reach of Scotland, you could also try skiing on snow, at one of the mountain resorts.

You won't need to invest in loads of expensive equipment just to have a go at skiing. Tracksuit-type clothes and gloves, with something waterproof if necessary, are fine. If you're an absolute beginner - like me - it's essential to have a lesson or two, but you'll soon get the hang of it! Even if you keep falling over at first, don't be embarrassed.

JUST LOOK AT THE UTTERLY BRILL EDDIE 'THE EAGLE' EDWARDS. HE WAS DREADFUL! BUT THAT DIDN'T STOP HIM FROM TAKING PART IN THE SKI-JUMP EVENT AT THE WINTER OLYMPICS!

If you're more daring than I am, there are several sports you can try on artificial slopes besides conventional downhill skiing. For the utterly reckless among you, slalom skiing involves swerving at high speed around a series of poles. If you're completely mad, you might enjoy mogul skiing - skiing through a series of bumps. But if you want to be completely up-to-the-minute, the latest craze in snow sports is snow boarding - a cross between surfing and skateboarding!

44

Did you know that a fish's speed depends on its length and the warmth of its body? Once, when a fisherman caught a cosmopolitan tail fish – the fastest fish in the world – it took 91 metres of fishing line in 3 seconds. This means it was swimming at over 100km per hour. Personally I prefer to lie still. . .

Make a lot of BRILL meringues

To make loads of really taste-tastic meringues, you'll need:

* 5 egg whites
* 25 g brown sugar
* a quarter of a teaspoon of salt
* ingredients for fillings

A VERY STRONG ARM FOR A LOT OF WHISKING!

BRILL TIP

To separate the white of an egg from the yolk, you have to crack the egg, and carefully let the white drain away until there's only the yolk left in the broken shell. This is a bit tricky at first, so it's best to do each one over a separate bowl. This way, if some yolk escapes into the white, you'll only waste one egg, not the whole lot! It's really important not to let any yolk fall into the whites, otherwise they won't whisk up.

1 Prepare a baking tray by brushing some oil over it and then laying a piece of greaseproof paper over it. Turn the oven on to Gas mark 4/350°F to heat up.

2 Now whisk all the egg whites together, adding the sugar a little bit at a time, until the mixture is really smooth and frothy. Then add the salt, whisk again until the mixture becomes firm and stands up in stiff peaks when you lift the whisk out of it. (It takes loads of whisking to get the mixture really stiff, so if yours is still quite runny, keep at it! It'll thicken up eventually... well, if your arm doesn't drop off first...)

3 Spoon the whisked egg whites onto the baking sheet in little heaps, making sure that there's space in between them.

4 Bake them in the oven for about 25 - 30 minutes, until they're dry and crisp. Take them out of the oven and leave them to cool down.

I personally think they're yummy just as they are, but if you can keep your hands off them long enough, you can sandwich them together with different fillings. Try fresh fruit and cream, or fruit purées like banana and raspberry, or apple purée with a sprinkling of cinammon.

What's white and fluffy and swings through the jungle?

A meringue-outang!

Jellyfish may make the best puddings but I tell the best jokes . . .

In 1860, an anonymous person sent out hundreds of invitations to a party to see the washing of the white lions at the Tower of London on April the first. People did actually turn up!

Did you know that although ice hockey players wear so much safety gear that they look like storm troopers, the game is so rough that players are continually substituted. They're usually on the ice for no longer than two minutes at a time. And people call me wet!

Tenpin Bowling is Dead

BRILL

(O)ne of the best things about bowling is that anyone can do it! (Well, almost anyone. Fish can't, of course...Sorry, Brill.)

Modern-style tenpin bowling comes from America - it's even rumoured that there are three specially-built bowling lanes underneath the White House! But the roots of the game go back much further than that ...

Who invented tenpin bowling?

Bowling was the most popular game in Elizabethan England. In fact, it was so popular that it became known as 'the commoners' sport' - although as Sir Francis Drake himself had to be interrupted playing bowls to go and defeat the Spanish Armada, it couldn't have been all that common!

It's actually thought that bowling is in fact more than 7000 years old, as skittles were found in the grave of an Egyptian child who was buried around 5200 BC!

How to play

The rules of tenpin bowling are dead easy. You get two tries to try to knock over ten pins with a bowling ball, and you get ten goes overall. But it's not quite as simple as it sounds - I couldn't even work out which fingers to hold the bowling ball with! (It's your middle two fingers and your thumb, in fact.) If you're dead BRILL and knock over all ten pins in a single bowl, it's called a strike. But if the ball rolls straight into the gutter at the side of the bowling lane and misses all the pins, it's called a gutterball - or even a 'John Eccleston'!

Don't try to do anything fancy at first, just keep your feet facing forwards and try to bowl the ball straight forwards, with a smooth underarm action. Oh, don't forget the most important thing of all -

REMEMBER TO LET GO!

Many bowling centres have a club you can join. If you get really BRILL, there are also competition leagues throughout the year. Some bowling alleys will even arrange a birthday party for you (although you have to bring your own mates). And if you can't be bothered to drag yourself out of the house, you can always play the couch-potato version of bowling with ten plastic bottles on your living room floor.

INFO

If a predator gets hold of a lizard's tail, the tail snaps off and starts wriggling around, to fool the predator into thinking that it's caught its supper. Meanwhile, the lizard legs it in the opposite direction - alive, but minus its tail! The tail does grow back, but it takes quite a while...

Oh no! Not again...

How to be a BRILL TV presenter

> So you think you're a budding Brucie?

> You reckon you've got the energy to be the next Anneka Rice?

> BUT HAVE YOU GOT THE CHARM, TALENT, SOPHISTICATION AND GOOD LOOKS YOU NEED TO PRESENT BRILL?

> He's talking about me, of course!

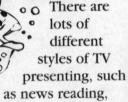

There are lots of different styles of TV presenting, such as news reading, game show hosting, roving reporting and chat show interviewing - to name but a few! There's also the BRILL style of TV presenting, where your co-host is actually a fish. In any case, presenting skills are useful for lots of situations, whether you're introducing a school concert, doing a bit of acting, or maybe even going for an interview. You need to be confident, well-prepared and ready for anything!

How to be BRILL at newsreading

Firstly, the most important newsreading tip is

DON'T PANIC!

This is because the news has to be completely up-to-the-minute, so it often changes at the very last second - sometimes even when you're on air!

Secondly, the script for the news appears under the TV camera on a special screen called an Autocue (we can't afford this at BRILL, so we just write our script onto large cards) so it takes lots and lots of practice to be able to read it while looking into the camera at the same time - unless you've naturally got one eye higher than the other, like Brill!

Thirdly, no matter what your own opinions are about what you're reading, you mustn't let the viewers at home get any idea of what you think.

"EC officials are forcing up the price of British fish and chips by an average of 50p ..."

That's outrageous! I look forward to my fish and chip supper on Thursdays ...

Finally, all the best newsreaders finish by pressing a few computer keys. It doesn't matter what you type, as the studio crew does all the technical stuff. The important thing is to look efficient and as if you know what you're doing.

How to be **BRIL** at presenting: breakfast TV

This one isn't for you if you like a lie-in in the mornings! No one wants to wake up to someone who looks as if they've only just peeled off their pyjamas. Besides this, it's no good if you're still half-asleep, as presenting live means you have to be alert, and prepared for anything to happen.

No matter what you got up to the night before, you have to be bright, happy and relaxed - wearing casual clothes and sitting on a squashy sofa definitely helps. A good way to keep conversation going without

rIse aNd SHiNE!

waffffling is to ask questions to your guests. But the most important tip is to be incredibly nice and suck up to your crew, as they have the power to make you look completely stupid in front of millions of people!

How to be a **BRILL** game show host

In the wonderful world of light entertainment, the game show host is king. I mean this quite literally, because all TV game show hosts seem to be male! This doesn't mean that if you're a girl and you're sure that your vocation in life is to present 'Grab As Much As You Can!', that you can't do it. Someone has to be the first ever female game show host, so why shouldn't it be you?

(Besides which, it's a good excuse to get to know gorgeous Gary from next door by asking him to be your male assistant while you practise.)

The most BRILL game show hosts give their contestants the space they need to be themselves. It also helps if you remember their names. But to make it as a game show host legend, you'll need your own gimmick (like a funny walk or a wig) or catchphrase, so people can imitate you.

How to be **BRILL** at commentating

There are two main styles of commentating: one is used only for horse racing, where you have to speak so quickly that it doesn't matter what you say, as no one can understand you anyway; the other is for sporting events in general.

and they're off...

The essential skill to master is holding the lip mike under your nose.

Remember that viewers rely on your voice to describe the action, because they can't see you. It's up to you to create atmosphere and suspense by what you say and how you say it. If there's lots of action, you can get quite excited.

If there's no action, then you can describe what's going on around you, or even tell funny stories about things that have happened to you and your friends. It doesn't matter if you get your words mixed up, as you can always make lots of money later by writing a book about the funny things you said by accident.

Survival tips for pop star interviews

The biggest problem about interviewing pop stars is where to find a pop star to interview. This involves a lot of patience and detective work.

Once you've managed to track one down, and you've successfully attracted their attention or bribed/sneaked your way into their presence, interviewing a pop star can be hard-going, as they're often completely mad. If you're unlucky enough to get a really difficult pop star, they might just answer 'yes' or 'no' to all your questions.

On the other hand, a pop star might do a lot of talking, but only want to talk about things you haven't had time to research, and so know nothing about.

So to survive a pop interview, it's best to prepare the first words and the last words you're going to say, and be ready to bluff your way through anything that happens in between. You can try to make conversation by asking the pop star to tell you about their new album or tour, or to explain why they wrote a certain song, but don't blame me if this doesn't work!
Good luck!

Did you know?

Did you know that the drivers of London black taxi-cabs have BRILL memories? They have to learn the whereabouts of every single street, restaurant, hotel and theatre before they can get their driving licence. By my calculation, there are over 50,000 streets in London! Cabbies call this 'The Knowledge'.
I call it mind-blowing!

BRAIN 1

13392

Be BRILL at mini-modelling

Way back in the mists of time, humans made household goods from the very earth beneath their feet. And even though we can now go out and buy cooking pots in all shapes and sizes, the creative urge to express ourselves remains deep within us. Why not release this artistic impulse by the means of mini-modelling?

Loads of people are mad about modelling fish, because it's such an easy thing to get hooked on.

There are special kinds of modelling material you can buy which are all easier and cleaner to work with than clay. You just warm a small bit in your hand until it's very pliable, and you're off ... These materials also come in different colours, so you don't have to mess around trying to paint your model. Modelling materials can be cooked in an oven and made permanent.

(ALWAYS FOLLOW THE INSTRUCTIONS ON THE PACKET.
IT WOULD BE A REAL SHAME FOR YOUR MINI-MODELLING TALENTS
TO BE NIPPED IN THE BUD ALL BECAUSE YOU BLEW UP
YOUR MUM'S ELECTRIC OVEN.)

Make your own modelling dough

If you don't want to buy special modelling materials, you can make your own modelling dough at home. Just mix one cup of salt with two cups of flour and add enough water so that when you mix it all up it turns into a gooey, sticky dough. Bang it around a bit on a breadboard for a while, until it's nice and pliable. Then you can mould it into whatever you like and bake it in the oven to harden it. A word of warning - even though this dough goes a nice golden-brown colour when it's baked, don't try to eat your models. They taste revolting. (Don't ask how I found this out...)

What to model?

The only limit to modelling is your imagination, as you can make anything with practice and patience. Try making teddies, strings of beads, food, carnivorous plants, racing cars, magical monsters - anything is possible! If you're not very good with your fingers, you can always use cut out flat shapes and letters to make patterned brooches or name badges. If you're going to use pastry cutters, remember to use them on a cutting board. I don't want to be the one your mum blames when you make pretty patterns into the surface of her mahogany dining table. And always be very careful when using sharp modelling tools - even experts have been known to slice off the tops of their fingers. Besides being incredibly painful, this also tends to ruin their models, as everything gets stained red...

INFO

The Thames has frozen over thick enough for people to skate on it a total of nine times. In 1814 a frost fair was held on the ice between Blackfriars Bridge and London Bridge. There wasn't just skating, there was also dancing, skittles and horse races, whole sheep were roasted, and some idiot even lit a huge bonfire.

FROST FAIR

What lies at the bottom of the sea and shivers?
A nervous wreck.

BRILL pop stardom

So you think you could be bigger than the Beatles, Tina Turner and Bruce Springsteen - all rolled into one? The music industry might look really glamorous, but surviving in a pop group is far from easy! There's so much competition that it's not enough just to be BRILL! You also need bucketfuls of determination, energy and enthusiasm, and you have to be prepared to put in lashings of hard work. If you still want to try the wonderful world of pop, read on ...

Putting together your band

1 To find the members of your band, you need to hold an audition. Make some posters to advertise it, so you get as many hopefuls as possible to choose from.

2 Apart from looking for musical talent, it's just as important to pick people who aren't going to hate each other! It isn't worth having even the most BRILL bass player in your town if his pop star-sized ego makes you all want to bash up his guitar.

3 It also helps if you all want to put the same amount of time and energy into the group, and all like similar musical styles.

The first hurdle is to decide on a good name. Agreeing on a name usually causes so many arguments that if your band makes it past this one, you've got a fair to middling chance of staying together. You also need to work on getting a distinctive, easily-recognisable look.

How to be BRILL at songwriting:

The best songs are always about what people already know. It doesn't matter how boring your subject may seem in itself, it's your feelings on the subject that matter. I mean look at some of the things people have sung about - green doors, yellow ribbons and blue hotels to mention but a few. When you've thought of something you want to write your song about, it often helps to write down everything you can think of that has anything to do with the subject you've chosen. You'll then find it easier to form sentences and pick out rhymes.

How to make your own dead BRILL demo tape

All self-respecting bands have to make a demo tape of what they sound like. But you don't need to spend loads of dosh on an expensive recording studio. As long as you can lay your hands on a cassette recorder, you can easily make a recording of your group for yourself. Then your next step is ...

Landing a record deal

Do anything you can to get your band noticed! Stick up posters to advertise your gigs and try for support from your local radio station. You should also send your demo tape to record companies (look in Yellow Pages under 'record companies' to find some local names and addresses). But your presentation must be good enough to stand out and attract attention, as record companies receive hundreds of demo tapes every day! It's a good idea to include some information about the band - like how long you've been together, who the members are and what kind of style you play... If you can send a video of yourselves too, then all the better!

BRIL TIP

Remember that if anyone offers to manage your group, it doesn't mean you'll automatically get a recording deal. Some managers are dastardly villains who turn out to be more trouble than they're worth - so be careful!

My favourite band's Marillion - the lead singer's called 'Fish'.

Most importantly - don't give up! Madonna didn't get where she is today by throwing in the towel when she had a bad day ...

Did you know?

Did you know that Rory Blackwell from Devon has played the most instruments simultaneously? A record 108.

Did you also know that Happy Birthday is the most frequently sung song ever in the Universe? It was even sung in space by the Apollo astronauts, in 1969!

ROCK LOBSTERS

Be BRILL at impressions

Picking the right people to impersonate is really important when it comes to being BRILL at impressions. Let's face it, some people are just impossible to do impressions of because they're so boringly normal! (Unless you're John Major, in which case it's easy to impersonate you because you're normally so boring ...) People with individual mannerisms, an unusual voice, or distinctive physical features are the easiest to impersonate. But it's still down to you to observe every tiny detail of your subjects very closely and put in loads of practice.

Getting started

A good way to get started is to use your natural talents. If you naturally look like someone famous you're already half-way to a perfect impression of them, so why not work on them first. If you've got an accent (like Geordie, Liverpudlian, Irish etc), you might find it easy to impersonate a famous person from where you live. If you want to perfect an impression of someone on TV, try video recording them. This way you watch them over and over again - careful observation and lots of practice really are the only ways to get an impression just right.

Getting better

To get the look and mannerisms right, it's a really good idea to practise in front of a mirror. Using props will also make you look more like the person you're trying to imitate. These don't have to be expensive; you'll probably find just the wig, hat or spectacles you're looking for in charity second hand shops or car boot sales. To practice the voice, try recording yourself and playing it back - it's always surprising when you hear how you really sound to other people.

BEFORE YOU AUDITION FOR THE TV, SHOW YOUR IMPRESSION TO YOUR FAMILY AND FRIENDS. THEY MIGHT COME UP WITH SOME BRILL TIPS OF THEIR OWN.

IF AT FIRST YOU DON'T SUCCEED, TRY, TRY AND TRY AGAIN!

Don't worry if you can't get your impression absolutely perfect. A funny send-up can be just as BRILL.

INFO

All paper is valuable, because you have to chop down trees to make it! But paper with pictures of royalty and little numbers on obviously has a special value! Everyone's seen five or ten pound notes, but have you ever seen a million pound note? Deep within the vaults of the Bank of England there are in fact two real million pound notes! But they're never used outside the Bank of England. Who would have enough change for a million pound note, anyway?

Make a **BRILL** spinning piece of paper

Beat the Harlem Globetrotters at their own game! A sheet of airmail writing paper is best for this BRILL trick - your friends won't believe their eyes when you make a piece of paper spin on the tip of your forefinger!

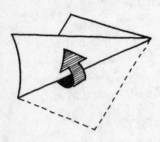 

1 Fold one corner of the paper across, to make a diagonal crease, then unfold the paper.

2 Turn the paper round and do the same for another diagonal.

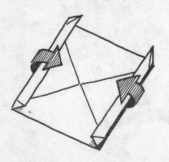 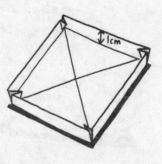

3 Open out the paper so it lies flat again, then fold all the edges over to a depth of one centimetre. Make strong creases, so the edges all stand up like a shallow tray. You'll have to squeeze the corners together, so everything holds together properly.

4 Place the middle of the paper - with the tray facing outwards - on your right forefinger, using your left hand to hold it in position (or vice versa, if you're left handed). Hold your arms out as straight as you can. Now turn around quickly, and let go with your left (or right!) hand. The paper will spin on the tip of your forefinger!

IT MAY TAKE A BIT OF
PRACTICE, BUT EVENTUALLY
YOU SHOULD BECOME SO
BRILL THAT YOU CAN KEEP
THE PAPER SPINNING FOR
QUITE A LONG TIME...

Make dead BRILL jacket potatoes

acket potatoes take a nanosecond to cook in the microwave, but they don't look or taste all that good. Alternatively, you can leave them for what seems like hours in the oven. They then look and taste better, but by the time they're ready you're probably not hungry anymore, as you always have to eat three packets of crisps while you wait for them to cook. But here's a way to make completely BRILL jacket potatoes - and it doesn't take forever.

You will need ...

* 34 million spuds
* a slab of butter
* half a ton of salt
* any toppings you like, including truck loads of cheese, buckets of baked beans, sweetcorn, peppers, a field of mushrooms, peanuts and GALLONS of Daddie's Sauce

1 Heat your oven up to gas mark 7/425°F/210°C.

2 Prick your jacket potatoes all over with a fork and cook them in a microwave, on the highest setting. Each jacket potato needs about 3 minutes on each side, so if you're making two, cook them for 6 minutes on each side; if you're making three, cook them for 9 minutes on each side; if you're making four, cook them for 12 minutes on each side; and so on ...

3 Next, brush them in a bit of oil (cooking oil, not car oil) and sprinkle some salt over them.

4 Pop them in the oven for about 45 minutes, until they're crispy on the outside but soft on the inside.

Instead of just dumping your filling on top of your perfectly-cooked jacket potato, try scooping out the potato - so you're left with two empty halves of potato skin - and mix it together with your fillings and a little butter. Then you can fill up the halves of potato skin again with the mixture. This way it doesn't just taste BRILL, it looks BRILL, too!

I think chefs are cruel - they beat eggs, whip cream and batter fish!

GRUB'S UP!

In 1648, England's ruling family, the Stuarts, were defeated by Oliver Cromwell and escaped to Europe. The future King James II didn't sit around twiddling his thumbs, however, but instead learnt how to skate. When he found himself back in ice rink-less London, he spent ages waiting for the river Thames to freeze over so he could show off how BRILL he was.

Did you know?

Did you know that the Australian burrowing toad can live without water for up to three years because of a special protective layer on its skin? And did you know that the most deadly animal in the world is the poison arrow frog? Just one millilitre of its poison can kill up to 4,000 people!

How to chat someone up and be **BRILL** at it

Chatting someone up is no problem if you follow the easy steps of this BRILL guide.
And remember, if the worst happens and they say 'no', there are plenty more fish in the sea...

BRILL preparations

1 First find someone you like.

2 Be yourself. There's no point in trying to be something you're not, because you'll never be able to keep it up! Just make the most of what you've got. It's no good unless the person you fancy likes you just the way you are - warts and all.

3 Wear something comfortable - if you're comfortable, you're going to feel good, and if you feel good, then you're going to look good.

4 Make sure you're not smelly! (A bit of soap and deodorant work wonders in this department.)

5 Most importantly of all, resist the urge to do anything disgusting like burp or pick your nose. First impressions last, remember!

6 Don't wait for them to ask you - DIY! Whether you're a boy or a girl, if you don't do the asking, you'll never find out if someone likes you or not. Besides which, if they say no, you can stop wasting your time and move on to someone else.

BRILL ways to break the ice

Even if you pluck up the courage to approach the object of your desire at school or at a party, you still need something devastatingly BRILL to say to them! Well, here are some 100% guaranteed chat-up lines.

1 Have you got ten pence? (The person will say 'yes'.) Well, give me a ring sometime.

2 Did you hear about the overweight polar bear? (The person will say 'no'.) No, neither did I, but it broke the ice, didn't it?

3 I'm writing a book on BRILL chat-up lines. Suppose you wanted to impress me, what would your best chat-up line be? (The person will then tell you a chat-up line. Whatever they say, here's your reply.) OK, I'm impressed. Take me - I'm yours.

4 This is my best chat up line – it works every time! Would you like a fish supper - me?

GO FOR IT!

When you ask someone out,
just make sure that you're prepared if they
say yes. You don't want to stand there with your
mouth wide open like a fish because you're so
shocked that they said yes in the first place!
Have some ideas up your sleeve about where
you could go
together.

A **BRIL** first date

Unfortunately, one thing you can be sure of is that - even if you've never had the tiniest pimple before - a **THROBBING BOIL** is bound to erupt on the end of your nose five minutes before your all-important first date. It's not going to be much comfort if I tell you that everyone gets spots at some time in their life, and there's not much you can do about it. At the end of the day, it's the personality behind the spots that really counts - and don't let anyone tell you otherwise!

You'll be able to tell if it's working because you'll be looking at each other with soft, fuzzy eyes and giggling nervously. (You may laugh, but wait until you fall for someone and watch yourself go completely mushy.) If, on the other hand, the object of your affection has their arms and legs crossed and is looking bored - forget it. Find someone else. After all, it's their problem if they can't recognise good looks, wit and charm when they see it!

Did you know that one of the best April Fool's jokes was in the 1950s, when a TV news programme convinced millions of viewers that there were spaghetti trees growing in Italy. What silly people!
(I still can't find out where spaghetti does grow, though.)

INFO

ndian snake charmers don't, in fact, hypnotise snakes with their music. For a start off, cobras are deaf, so they can't hear music anyway. And secondly, the snake follows the pipe backwards and forwards because it's watching the 'eye' of the pipe, and is getting ready to strike it.

Be dead **BRILL** at DIY video

Videos are definitely BRILL. But if you're like me, you'll know just what a hassle it is to choose which one you want to watch! (I have been known to get kicked out of the video shop for taking too long...)

RUN VT! EDIT

What lurks at the bottom of the sea and makes you an offer you can't refuse?

The Codfather.

Well, now you can get around that little problem by making your own. It's not as expensive as you'd think, and - apart from a video camera - you don't need lots of special equipment. You can get your finger on the button by borrowing a camcorder from a relative or friend. Many schools, youth groups and even local libraries will lend out equipment to young people who want to make their own films.

◀◀◀ REPLAY *action!*

DIY video dos and don'ts

1 Don't overuse the zoom! This has been known to make the people watching your video violently seasick as they focus in and out, in and out, in and ...

2 Use the mains adapter on your camcorder whenever possible, as it's a complete and utter pain when the battery pack runs out just as the star of your video is about to make their appearance.

3 Once you've got used to the camera, try some lighting effects. With a torch you can get BRILL shadows for horror movies or even a 'streetlighting' effect.

4 It's very useful to have a separate microphone which you can place as close to the scene as possible. The built-in microphone on a camcorder is often a long way from the action, so your sound might be poor if you just rely on this.

5 If you have one, use a tripod to keep your camcorder steady. This way, you'll avoid intriguing shots of the pavement.

6 If you're following a storyboard, try to edit in-camera. This means filming the scenes in the right order, so you don't have to mess about with editing afterwards.

7 Don't bore your family and friends with the 106th showing of 'Jess and Mitch's BRILL day out' - make another video!

Did you know?

To all who are struggling to do perfect impressions, did you know that I'm naturally a BRILL impressionist? My family - the flatfish - are coloured differently on either side. So when I turn pale-side down and lie on the sea bed, I look exactly like the sand and you can't see me. That's why I've got both eyes on one side of my head, too ...
You should be so lucky, eh?

In Scandinavia and Holland in the Middle Ages ice skating wasn't a hobby, it was a method of transport! People used to travel backwards and forwards along ice-covered canals and fjords on skates with iron blades. So now you know where the saying, 'get your skates on!' comes from.

The 1950s were BRILL

In the 1950s there was a brand new style for everything!

Al Tupper had the brilliant idea of inventing little plastic containers to keep things in, and everyone who was anyone held tupperware parties. Also the automobile came into its own, as for the first time it became affordable to own a car. Driving became a hobby. As far as design was concerned, the fifties was the era of the tail fin!

Now that's the car for me!

COOL

As for dancing, the latest fashion was the 'jive', where boy and girl partners used a base of six steps to create complicated and exciting moves together. But this wasn't the only dance around in the 1950s.

The 'madison' was the first of several 'line dances' in which gangs would dance their own routines. Others then had to see how good they were at picking them up and joining in! In the 'stroll', boys and girls formed two lines opposite each other and then 'strolled' down in between, dancing their favourite steps.

CONGA EELS

I've got two left feet, actually, but even so, dancing with a partner's still much more fun than bobbing up and down opposite someone, like we do today! By the way, did you know that the 'moon walk' actually has its roots in a 1950s' dance? James Brown took a step called the 'camel walk' and started doing it backwards, then Michael Jackson renamed it as the moon walk! Did you also know that the juke box got its name because in 1930s America the word 'juke' meant 'dance'? So now you know.

WHAT ARE YOU SITTING THERE FOR? GET JUKING!

Fish
Hook

Why has this page got 'Fish Hook' written on it?

Because it's the end of the line.